T0198464

RICHES
ARE YOUR
RIGHT

Maple Spring Publishing Titles

PRINT, EPUB & AUDIO

Crystallizing Public Opinion

Think and Grow Rich

The Richest Man in Babylon

The Power of Your Subconscious Mind

The Magic of Believing

The Science of Getting Rich

The Prince

Letters from a Stoic

The Mystery of the Blue Train

The Dynamic Laws of Prosperity

The Great Gatsby

How to Attract Money with Bonus

Riches Are Your Right with Bonus

This is It with Bonus

Quiet Moments With God with Bonus

EPUB & AUDIO

The Art of War

The Science of Being Great

Your Invisible Power

At Your Command

The Magic Story

Think and Grow Rich Deluxe Original Edition

T.N.T.: It Rocks the Earth

Believe in Yourself

How to Use the Power of Prayer

This is It

Quiet Moments with God

The Power of Your Subconscious Mind with Bonus

The Greatest thing in the World

ORIGINAL CLASSIC EDITION

RICHES ARE YOUR RIGHT

FEATURES BONUS BOOK: HOW TO USE THE POWER OF PRAYER

JOSEPH MURPHY

MAPLE SPRING PUBLISHING

Published 2024 by Maple Spring Publishing

Front cover design by David Rheinhardt of Pyrographx

Interior design by Meghan Day Healey of Story Horse, LLC.

Library of Congress Cataloging-in-Publication Data is available upon request

ISBN: 979-8-3505-0069-1

10 9 8 7 6 5 4 3 2 1

Contents

1 Consciousness of Health...................................7

2 Accept Abundance...15

3 Love, Personality, Human and
   Family Relationships... 23

4 Expression... 31

BONUS: How to Use the Power of Prayer 43

About the Author 73

1

Consciousness of Health

How to Apply the Healing Principle

I will restore health unto thee, and I will heal thee of thy wounds, saith the Lord." The God in me has limitless possibilities. I know that all things are possible with God. I believe this and accept it whole-heartedly now. I know that the God-Power in me makes darkness light and crooked things straight. I am now lifted up in consciousness by contemplating that God indwells me.

I speak the word now for the healing of mind, body, and affairs; I know that this Principle within me responds to my faith and trust. "The Father doeth the works." I am now in touch with life, love, truth, and beauty within me. I now align myself with the Infinite Principle of Love and Life within me. I know that harmony, health, and peace are now being expressed in my body.

As I live, move, and act in the assumption of my perfect health, it becomes actual. I now imagine and feel the reality of my perfect body. I am filled with a sense of peace and well-being. Thank you, Father.

Prayer for Health

—❧•❧—

Jesus said, "Thy faith hath made thee whole."
    I positively believe in the Healing Power of God within me. My conscious and subconscious mind are in perfect agreement. I accept the statement of truth which I positively affirm. The words I speak are words of spirit and they are truth.

I now decree that the Healing Power of God is transforming my whole body making me whole, pure, and perfect. I believe with a deep, inner certitude that my prayer of faith is being manifest now. I am guided by the Wisdom of God in all matters. The Love of God flows in transcendent beauty and loveliness into my mind and body, transforming, restoring, and energizing every atom of my being. I sense the peace that passeth understanding. God's Glory surrounds me, and I rest forever in the Everlasting Arms.

Wearing His Garment

—❧•❧—

I have found God in the sanctuary of my own soul. God is Life; that Life is my life. I know God is not a body; He is shapeless, timeless, and ageless; I see God in my mind's eye. Through understanding I see and look upon God in the same way that I see the answer to a mathematical problem.

I now rise to the awareness of peace, poise, and power. This feeling of joy, peace, and goodwill within me is actually the Spirit of God moving within me; It is God in action; It is Almighty. There is no power in external things to hurt me; the only Power resides in my own mind and consciousness.

My body is the garment of God. The Living Spirit Almighty is within me; It is absolutely pure, holy, and perfect. I know that this Holy Spirit is God, and that this Spirit is now flowing through me healing and making my body whole, pure, and perfect. I have complete power over my body and my world.

My thoughts of peace, power, and health have the Power of God to be realized within me now. "Blessed are the pure in heart: for they shall see God." I have seen and felt His Holy Presence; it is wonderful.

The Quiet Mind

God dwells at the center of my being. God is Peace; this Peace enfolds me in Its Arms now. There is a deep feeling of security, vitality, and strength underlying this peace. This inner sense of peace, in which I now dwell, is the Silent Brooding Presence of God. The Love and the Light of God watch over me, as a loving mother watches over the sleeping child. Deep in my heart is the Holy Presence that is my peace, my strength, and my source of supply.

All fear has vanished. I see God in all people; I see God manifest in all things. I am an instrument of the Divine Presence. I now release this inner peace; it flows through my entire being releasing and dissolving all problems; this is the peace that passeth understanding.

Mental Poise

Whither shall I go from thy Spirit? Or whither shall I flee from thy Presence? If I ascend up into heaven, thou art there: if I make my bed in hell, behold, thou art there. If I take the wings of the morning, and dwell in the uttermost parts of the sea: Even there shall thy hand lead me, and thy right hand shall hold me." I am now full of a Divine enthusiasm, because I am in the Presence of Divinity. I am in the Presence of All Power, Wisdom, Majesty, and Love.

The Light of God illumines my intellect; my mind is full of poise, balance, and equilibrium. There is a perfect mental adjustment to all things. I am at peace with my own thoughts. I rejoice in my work; it gives me joy and happiness. I draw continually upon my Divine Storehouse; for It is the only Presence and the only Power. My mind is God's mind; I am at peace.

The Peace of God

All is peace and harmony in my world, for God in me is "The Lord of Peace." I am the consciousness of God in action; I am always at peace. My mind is poised, serene, and calm. In this atmosphere of peace and goodwill which surrounds me, I feel a deep abiding strength and freedom from all fear. I now sense and feel the love and beauty of His Holy Presence. Day by day I am more aware of God's Love; all that is false falls away. I see God personified in all people. I know that as I allow this inner peace to flow through my being, all problems are solved. I dwell in God; therefore, I rest in the eternal arms of peace. My life is the life of God. My peace is the deep, unchanging peace of God; "It is the peace of God, which passeth all understanding."

The Gift of God

—❧❧—

A merry heart maketh a cheerful countenance." The spirit of the Almighty pervades every atom of my being making me whole, joyous, and perfect. I know that all the functions of my body respond to this inner joy welling up within me. I am now stirring up the gift of God within me; I feel wonderful. The oil of joy and illumination anoint my intellect and become a lamp unto my feet.

I am now perfectly adjusted emotionally; there is a Divine equilibrium functioning in my mind, body, and affairs. I resolve from this moment forward to express peace and happiness to every person I meet. I know that my happiness and peace come from God; as I shed His light, love, and truth to others, I am also blessing and healing myself in countless ways. I radiate the sunshine of God's Love to all mankind. His Light shines through me and illuminates my path. I am resolved to express peace, joy, and happiness.

Controlling My Emotions

—❧❧—

When a negative thought of fear, jealousy, or resentment enters my mind, I supplant it with the thought of God. My thoughts are God's thoughts, and God's Power is with my thoughts of good. I know I have complete dominion over my thoughts and emotions. I am a channel of the Divine. I now redirect all my feelings and emotions along harmonious, constructive lines. "The sons of God shouted for joy." I now rejoice to accept the ideas of God which are peace, harmony, and goodwill and I delight to express them; this heals all discord within me. Only God's ideas enter my mind, bringing me harmony, health, and peace.

God is Love. Perfect Love casteth out fear, resentment, and all negative states. I now fall in love with truth. I wish for all men everything I wish for myself; I radiate love, peace, and goodwill to all. I am at peace.

Overcoming Fear

❧⋅❧

There is no fear, as "perfect Love casteth out fear." Today I permit Love to keep me in perfect harmony and peace with all levels of my world. My thoughts are loving, kind, and harmonious. I sense my oneness with God, for "In Him I live, move, and have my being."

I know that all my desires will be realized in perfect order. I trust the Divine Law within me to bring my ideals to pass. "The Father doeth the works." I am divine, spiritual, joyous, and absolutely fearless. I am now surrounded by the perfect peace of God; it is "The peace of God which passeth all understanding." I now place all my attention on the thing desired. I love this desire and I give it my whole-hearted attention.

My spirit is lifted into the mood of confidence and peace; this is the spirit of God moving in me. It gives me a sense of peace, security, and rest. Truly, "perfect Love casteth out fear."

The Holy Temple

"Those that be planted in the house of the LORD shall flourish in the courts of our God." I am still and at peace. My heart and my mind are motivated by the spirit of goodness, truth, and beauty. My thought is now on the Presence of God within me; this stills my mind.

I know that the way of creation is Spirit moving upon Itself. My True Self now moves in and on Itself creating peace, harmony, and health in my body and affairs. I am Divine in my deeper self. I know I am a son of the living God; I create the way God creates by the self-contemplation of spirit. I know my body does not move of itself. It is acted upon by my thoughts and emotions.

I now say to my body, "Be still and quiet." It must obey. I understand this and I know it is a Divine Law. I take my attention away from the physical world; I feast in the House of God within me. I meditate and feast upon harmony, health, and peace; these come forth from the God-Essence within; I am at peace. My body is a temple of the Living God. "God is in His Holy Temple; let all the earth keep silent before Him."

2

Accept Abundance

God is the Eternal Now

(Using The Subconscious Mind)

I know that my good is this very moment. I believe in my heart that I can prophesy for myself harmony, health, peace, and joy. I enthrone the concept of peace, success, and prosperity in my mind now. I know and believe these thoughts (seeds) will grow and manifest themselves in my experience.

I am the gardener; as I sow, so shall I reap. I sow God-like thoughts (seeds); these wonderful seeds are peace, success, harmony, and goodwill. It is a wonderful harvest.

From this moment forward I am depositing in the Universal Bank (my subconscious mind) seeds or thoughts of peace, confidence, poise, and balance. I am drawing out the fruit of the wonderful seeds I am depositing. I believe and accept the fact that my desire is a seed deposited in the subconscious. I make it real by feeling the reality of it. I accept the reality of my desire in the same manner I accept the fact that the seed deposited in the ground will grow. I know it grows in the darkness; also, my desire or ideal grows in the darkness of my subconscious mind; in a little while, like the seed, it comes above the ground (becomes objectified) as a condition, circumstance, or event.

Infinite Intelligence governs and guides me in all ways. I meditate on whatsoever things are true, honest, just, lovely, and of good report. I think on these things, and God's Power is with my thoughts of Good. I am at peace.

The Way of Prayer

❧❦

Thou shalt make thy way prosperous, and then thou shalt have good success." I now give a pattern of success and prosperity to the deeper mind within me, which is the law. I now identify myself with the Infinite Source of supply. I listen to the still, small voice of God within me. This inner voice leads, guides, and governs all my activities. I am one with the abundance of God. I know and believe that there are new and better ways of conducting my business; Infinite Intelligence reveals the new ways to me.

I am growing in wisdom and understanding. My business is God's business. I am Divinely prospered in all ways. Divine Wisdom within me reveals the ways and means by which all my affairs are adjusted in the right way immediately.

The words of faith and conviction which I now speak open up all the necessary doors or avenues for my success and prosperity. I know that "The Lord (Law) will perfect that which concerneth me." My feet are kept in the perfect path, because I am a son of the living God.

How to Realize the Abundant Life

I know that *to prosper* means to grow spiritually along all lines. God is prospering me now in mind, body, and affairs. God's ideas constantly unfold within me bringing to me health, wealth, and perfect Divine expression.

I thrill inwardly as I feel the Life of God vitalizing every atom of my being. I know that God's Life is animating, sustaining, and strengthening me now. I am now expressing a perfect, radiant body full of vitality, energy, and power.

My business or profession is a Divine activity, and since it is God's business, it is successful and prosperous. I imagine and feel an inner wholeness functioning through my body, mind, and affairs. I give thanks and rejoice in the abundant life.

The Prayer of Faith

The prayer of faith shall save the sick and God shall raise him up." I know that no matter what the negation of yesterday was, that my prayer or affirmation of truth will rise triumphantly over it today. I steadfastly behold the joy of the answered prayer. I walk all day long in the Light.

Today is God's day; it is a glorious day for me, as it is full of peace, harmony, and joy. My faith in the good is written in my heart and felt in my inward parts. I am absolutely convinced that there is a Presence and a perfect Law which receives the impress of my desire now and which irresistibly attracts into my experience all the good things my heart desires. I now place all my reliance, faith, and trust in the Power and Presence of God within me; I am at peace.

I know I am a guest of the Infinite, and that God is my Host. I hear the invitation of the Holy One saying, "Come unto me all ye that labor, and I will give you rest." I rest in God; all is well.

The Abundant Life

C onsider the Lilies of the field; they toil not, neither do they spin; yet Solomon in all of his glory was not arrayed as one of these." I know that God is prospering me in all ways. I am now leading the abundant life, because I believe in a God of abundance. I am supplied with everything that contributes to my beauty, well being, progress, and peace. I am daily experiencing the fruits of the spirit of God within me; I accept my good now; I walk in the light that all good is mine. I am peaceful, poised, serene, and calm. I am one with the source of life; all my needs are met at every moment of time and every point of space. I now bring "all the empty vessels" to the Father within. The fullness of God is made manifest in all the departments of my life. "All that the Father hath is mine." I rejoice that this is so.

Imagination, the Workshop of God

W here there is no vision, the people perish." My vision is that I desire to know more of God and the way He works. My vision is for perfect health, harmony, and peace. My vision is the inner faith that Infinite Spirit leads and guides me now in all ways. I know and believe that the God-Power within me answers my prayer; this is a deep conviction within me.

I know that the mental picture to which I remain faithful will be developed in my subconscious mind and come forth on the screen of space.

I make it my daily practice to imagine only for myself and others that which is noble, wonderful, and God-like. I now imagine that I am doing the thing I long to do; I imagine that I now possess the things I long to possess; I imagine I am what I long to be. To make it real, I feel the reality of it; I know that it is so. Thank you, Father.

God's Will for Me

❧❧

God opens for me the windows of heaven, and pours me out a blessing."

God's will must be God-like; for that is the nature of God. God's will for me, therefore, is health, goodness, harmony, and abundance.

"If ye abide in me, and my words abide in you, ye shall ask what ye will, and it shall be done unto you." I am now enlightened by the truth; each day I am growing in wisdom and understanding. I am a perfect channel for the works of God; I am free from all worry and confusion. Infinite Intelligence within me is a lamp unto my feet. I know I am led to do the right thing; for it is God in action in all of my affairs.

The peace that passeth understanding fills my mind now. I believe and accept my ideal. I know it subsists in the Infinite. I give it form and expression by my complete mental acceptance. I feel the reality of the fulfilled desire. The peace of God fills my soul.

Abide in the Silence

Jesus said, "God is a Spirit: and they that worship him must worship him in spirit and in truth."

I know and realize that God is a spirit moving within me. I know that God is a feeling or deep conviction of harmony, health, and peace within me; it is the movement of my own heart. The spirit or feeling of confidence and faith which now possesses me is the spirit of God and the action of God on the waters of my mind; this is God; it is the creative Power within me.

I live, move, and have my being in the faith and confidence that goodness, truth, and beauty shall follow me all of the days of my life; this faith in God and all things good is omnipotent; it removes all barriers.

I now close the door of the senses; I withdraw all attention from the world. I turn within to the One, the Beautiful, and the Good; here, I dwell with my Father beyond time and space; here, I live, move, and dwell in the shadow of the Almighty. I am free from all fear, from the verdict of the world, and the appearance of things. I now feel His Presence which is the feeling of the answered prayer, or the presence of my good.

I become that which I contemplate. I now feel that I am what I want to be; this feeling or awareness is the action of God in me; it is the creative Power. I give thanks for the joy of the answered prayer and I rest in the silence that "It is done."

To Be, to Do, and to Have

At the center of my being is Peace; this is the peace of God. In this stillness I feel strength, guidance, and the love of His Holy Presence. I am Divinely active; I am expressing the fullness of God along all lines. I am a channel for the Divine, and I now release the imprisoned splendor that is within. I am Divinely guided to my true expression in life; I am compensated in a wonderful way. I see God in everything and personified in all men everywhere. I know as I permit this river of peace to flow through my being, all my problems are solved. All things I need to fully express myself on this plane are irresistibly attracted to me by the Universal Law of attraction. The way is revealed to me; I am full of joy and harmony.

Love, Personality, Human and Family Relationships

God's Broadcast

All ye are brethren, for one is your father." I always bring har-mony, peace, and joy into every situation and into all of my personal relationships. I know, believe, and claim that the peace of God reigns supreme in the mind and heart of everyone in my home and business. No matter what the problem is, I always main-tain peace, poise, patience, and wisdom. I fully and freely forgive everyone, regardless of what they may have said or done. I cast all my burdens on the God-self within; I go free; this is a marvelous feeling. I know that blessings come to me as I forgive.

I see the angel of God's Presence behind every problem or dif-ficult situation. I know the solution is there and that everything is working out in Divine order. I trust the God-Presence implicitly; it has the *know-how* of accomplishment. The Absolute Order of Heaven and His Absolute Wisdom are acting through me now and at all times; I know that order is Heaven's first law.

My mind is now fixed joyously and expectantly on this perfect harmony. I know the result is the inevitable, perfect solution; my answer is God's answer; it is Divine; for it is the melody of God's broadcast.

Spiritual Rebirth

⋟•⋞

Today I am reborn spiritually! I completely detach myself from the old way of thinking and I bring Divine love, light, and truth definitely into my experience. I consciously feel love for everyone I meet. Mentally I say to everyone I contact, "I see the God in you and I know you see the God in me." I recognize the qualities of God in everyone. I practice this morning, noon, and night; it is a living part of me.

I am reborn spiritually now, because all day long I practice the Presence of God. No matter what I am doing,—whether I am walking the street, shopping, or about my daily business,—whenever my thought wanders away from God or the good, I bring it back to the contemplation of His Holy Presence. I feel noble, dignified, and God-like. I walk in a high mood sensing my oneness with God. His peace fills my soul.

Love Frees

God is Love, and God is Life; this Life is one and indivisible. Life manifests Itself in and through all people; It is at the center of my own being.

I know that light dispels the darkness, so does the love of the good overcome all evil. My knowledge of the power of Love overcomes all negative conditions now. Love and hate cannot dwell together. I now turn the Light of God upon all fear or anxious thoughts in my mind, and they flee away. The dawn (light of truth) appears and the shadows (fear and doubt) flee away.

I know Divine Love watches over me, guides me, and makes clear the path for me. I am expanding into the Divine. I am now expressing God in all my thoughts, words, and actions; the nature of God is Love. I know that "perfect Love casteth out fear."

The Secret Place

He that dwelleth in the secret place of the most High shall abide under the shadow of the Almighty."

I dwell in the secret place of the most High; this is my own mind. All the thoughts entertained by me conform to harmony, peace, and goodwill. My mind is the dwelling place of happiness, joy, and a deep sense of security. All the thoughts that enter my mind contribute to my joy, peace, and general welfare. I live, move, and have my being in the atmosphere of good fellowship, love, and unity.

All the people that dwell in my mind are God's children. I am at peace in my mind with all the members of my household and all mankind. The same good I wish for myself, I wish for all men. I am living in the house of God now. I claim peace and happiness, for I know I dwell in the house of the Lord forever.

Overcoming Irritation

He that is slow to wrath, is of great understanding: but *he that* is hasty of spirit exalteth folly." I am always poised, serene, and calm. The peace of God floods my mind and my whole being. I practice the Golden Rule and sincerely wish peace and goodwill to all men.

I know that the love of all things which are good penetrates my mind casting out all fear. I am now living in the joyous expectancy of the best. My mind is free from all worry and doubt. My words of truth now dissolve every negative thought and emotion within me. I forgive everyone; I open the doorway of my heart to God's Presence. My whole being is flooded with the light and understanding from within.

The petty things of life no longer irritate me. When fear, worry, and doubt knock at my door, faith in goodness, truth, and beauty opens the door, and there is no one there. O, God, thou art my God, and there is none else.

Prayer of Gratitude

O give thanks unto the Lord; call upon His name; make known His deeds among the people. Sing unto him, sing psalms unto him: talk ye of all his wondrous works. Glory ye in His holy name: let the heart of them rejoice that seek the Lord."

I give thanks sincerely and humbly for all the goodness, truth, and beauty which flow through me. I have a grateful, uplifted heart for all the good that has come to me in mind, body, and affairs. I radiate love and goodwill to all mankind. I lift them up in my thought and feeling. I always show my gratitude and give thanks for all my blessings. The grateful heart brings my mind and heart in intimate union with the creative Power of the Cosmos. My thankful and exalted state of mind leads me along the ways by which all good things come.

"Enter into his gates with thanksgiving, and into his courts with praise: Be thankful unto him, and bless his name."

How to Attract the Ideal Husband

I know that I am one with God now. In Him I live, move, and have my being. God is Life; this life is the life of all men and women. We are all sons and daughters of the one Father.

I know and believe there is a man waiting to love and cherish me. I know I can contribute to his happiness and peace. He loves my ideals, and I love his ideals. He does not want to make me over; neither do I want to make him over. There is mutual love, freedom, and respect.

There is one mind; I know him now in this mind. I unite now with the qualities and attributes that I admire and want expressed by my husband. I am one with them in my mind. We know and love each other already in Divine Mind. I see the God in him; he sees the God in me. Having met him *within,* I must meet him in the *without;* for this is the law of my own mind.

These words go forth and accomplish whereunto they are sent. I know it is now done, finished, and accomplished in God. Thank you, Father.

How to Attract the Ideal Wife

❧·❧

God is one and indivisible. In Him we love, move, and have our being. I know and believe that God indwells every person; I am one with God and with all people. I now attract the right woman who is in complete accord with me. This is a spiritual union, because it is the spirit of God functioning through the personality of someone with whom I blend perfectly. I know I can give to this woman love, light, and truth. I know I can make this woman's life full, complete, and wonderful.

I now decree that she possesses the following qualities and attributes; i.e., she is spiritual, loyal, faithful, and true. She is harmonious, peaceful, and happy. We are irresistibly attracted to each other. Only that which belongs to love, truth, and wholeness can enter my experience. I accept my ideal companion now.

Divine Freedom

I f ye continue in my word, then are ye my disciples indeed: And ye shall know the truth, and the truth shall make you free." I know the truth, and the truth is that the realization of my desire would free me from all sense of bondage. I accept my freedom; I know it is already established in the Kingdom of God.

I know that all things in my world are projections of my inner attitudes. I am transforming my mind by dwelling on whatsoever things are true, lovely, noble, and God-like. I contemplate myself now as possessing all the good things of Life, such as peace, harmony, health, and happiness.

My contemplation rises to the point of acceptance; I accept the desires of my heart completely. God is the only Presence. I am expressing the fullness of God now. I am free! There is peace in my home, heart, and in all my affairs.

4

Expression

Prayer for World Peace

Peace begins with me. The peace of God fills my mind; the spirit of goodwill goes forth from me to all mankind. God is everywhere and fills the hearts of all men. In absolute truth all men are now spiritually perfect; they are expressing God's qualities and attributes. These qualities and attributes are Love, Light, Truth, and Beauty.

There are no separate nations. All men belong to the One Country—the One Nation which is God's Country. A country is a dwelling place; I dwell in the Secret Place of the Most High; I walk and talk with God—so do all men everywhere. There is only One Divine Family, and that is humanity.

There are no frontiers or barriers between nations, because God is One; God is indivisible. God cannot be divided against

Himself. The love of God permeates the hearts of all men every-where. His Wisdom rules and guides the nation; He inspires our leaders and the leaders of all nations to do His will, and His will only. The peace of God which passeth all understanding fills my mind and the minds of all men throughout the cosmos. Thank you, Father, for Thy peace; it is done.

Predicting My Future

❧•☙

"Thou madest him to have dominion over the works of thy hands." I know that my faith in God determines my future. My faith in God means my faith in all things good. I unite myself now with true ideas and I know the future will be in the image and likeness of my habitual thinking. "As a man thinketh in his heart so is he." From this moment forward my thoughts are on: "Whatsoever things are true, whatsoever things are honest, whatsoever things are just, whatsoever things are lovely, and of good report;" day and night I meditate on these things and I know these seeds (thoughts) which I habitually dwell upon will become a rich harvest for me. I am the captain of my own soul; I am the master of my fate; for my thought and feeling are my destiny.

My Destiny

❧•☙

I know that I mold, fashion, and create my own destiny. My faith in God is my destiny; this means an abiding faith in all things good. I live in the joy-out expectancy of the best; only the best comes to me. I know the harvest I will reap in the future, because all my thoughts are God's thoughts, and God is with my thoughts of good. My thoughts are the seeds of goodness, truth, and beauty. I now place my thoughts of love, peace, joy, success, and goodwill in the garden of my mind. This is God's garden and it will yield an abundant harvest. The glory and beauty of God will be expressed in my life. From this moment forward, I express life, love, and truth. I am radiantly happy and prosperous in all ways. Thank you, Father.

Impregnating the Subconscious Mind

❧

The first step in the mental acceptance of your idea, desire, or image is to relax, immobilize the attention, get still, and quiet. This quiet, relaxed, peaceful attitude of mind prevents extraneous matter and false ideas from interfering with the mental absorption of your ideal; furthermore in the quiet, passive, receptive attitude of mind effort is reduced to a minimum. In this relaxed manner affirm slowly and quietly several times a day the following:

> *"The perfection of God is now being expressed through me. The idea of health is now filling my subconscious mind. The image God has of me is a perfect image, and my subconscious mind recreates my body in perfect accordance to the perfect image held in the mind of God."*

This is a simple, easy way of conveying the idea of perfect health to your subconscious mind.

The Balanced Mind

❧❦❧

"Thou wilt keep him in perfect peace whose mind is stayed on thee, because he trusteth in thee." I know that the inner desires of my heart come from God within me. God wants me to be happy. The will of God for me is life, love, truth, and beauty. I mentally accept my good now and I become a perfect channel for the Divine.

I come into His Presence singing; I enter into His courts with praise; I am joyful and happy; I am still and poised.

The Still Small Voice whispers in my ear revealing to me my perfect answer. I am an expression of God. I am always in my true place doing the thing I love to do. I refuse to accept the opinions of man as truth. I now turn within and I sense and feel the rhythm of the Divine. I hear the melody of God whispering its message of love to me.

My mind is God's mind, and I am always reflecting Divine wisdom and Divine intelligence. My brain symbolizes my capacity to think wisely and spiritually. God's ideas unfold within my mind with perfect sequence. I am always poised, balanced, serene, and calm; for I know that God will always reveal to me the perfect solution to all my needs.

The Creative Word

❧❦❧

"Be ye doers of the word, and not hearers only, deceiving your own selves." My creative word is my silent conviction that my prayer is answered. When I speak the word for healing, success, or prosperity, my word is spoken in the consciousness of Life and Power, knowing that it is done. My word has power, because it is one with Omnipotence. The words I speak are always constructive and creative. When I pray, my words are full of life, love, and feeling; this makes my affirmations, thoughts, and words creative. I know the greater my faith behind the word spoken, the more power it has. The words I use form a definite mold, which determine what form my thought is to take. Divine Intelligence operates through me now and reveals to me what I need to know. I have the answer now. I am at peace. God is Peace.

The Scientific Prayer

Before they call, I will answer; and while they are yet speaking, I will hear."

When I pray, I call on the Father, the Son, and the Holy Ghost; the Father is my own consciousness; the Son is my desire; the Holy Ghost is the feeling of being what I want to be.

I now take my attention away from the problem, whatever it may be. My mind and heart are open to the influx from on High.

I know the Kingdom of God is within me. I sense, feel, understand, and know that my own life, my awareness of being, my own I Amness, is the Living Spirit Almighty. I now turn in recognition to this One Who Forever Is; the Light of God illumines my pathway; I am Divinely inspired and governed in all ways.

Now I begin to pray scientifically in order to bring my desire into manifestation by claiming and feeling myself to be and to have what I long to be and to have. I walk in the inner silent knowing of the soul, because I know my prayer is already answered, as I feel the reality of it in my heart. Thank you, Father; it is done!

The Divine Answer

I know that the answer to my problem lies in the God-Self within me. I now get quiet, still, and relaxed. I am at peace. I know God speaks in peace and not in confusion. I am now in tune with the Infinite; I know and believe implicitly that Infinite Intelligence is revealing to me the perfect answer. I think about the solution to my problems. I now live in the mood I would have were my problem solved. I truly live in this abiding faith and trust which is the mood of the solution; this is the spirit of God moving within me. This Spirit is Omnipotent; It is manifesting Itself; my whole being rejoices in the solution; I am glad. I live in this feeling and give thanks.

I know that God has the answer. With God all things are possible. God is the Living Spirit Almighty within me; He is the source of all wisdom and illumination.

The indicator of the Presence of God within me is a sense of peace and poise. I now cease all sense of strain and struggle; I trust the God-Power implicitly. I know that all the Wisdom and Power I need to live a glorious and successful life are within me. I relax my entire body; my faith is in His Wisdom; I go free. I claim and feel the peace of God flooding my mind, heart, and whole being. I know the quiet mind gets its problems solved. I now turn the request over to the God-Presence knowing It has an answer. I am at peace.

Prayer for Your Business

I now dwell on the Omnipresence and Omniaction of God. I know that this Infinite Wisdom guides the planets on their source. I know this same Divine Intelligence governs and directs all my affairs. I claim and believe Divine understanding is mine at all times. I know that all my activities are controlled by this indwelling Presence. All my motives are God-like and true. God's wisdom, truth, and beauty are being expressed by me at all times. The All-Knowing One within me knows what to do, and how to do it. My business or profession is completely controlled, governed, and directed by the love of God. Divine guidance is mine. I know God's answer, for my mind is at peace. I rest in the Everlasting Arms.

Right Action

I radiate goodwill to all mankind in thought, word, and deed. I know the peace and goodwill that I radiate to every man comes back to me a thousand fold. Whatever I need to know comes to me from the God-Self within me. Infinite Intelligence is operating through me revealing to me what I need to know. God in me knows only the answer. The perfect answer is made known to me now. Infinite Intelligence and Divine Wisdom make all decisions through me, and there is only right action and right expression taking place in my life. Every night I wrap myself in the Mantle of God's Love and fall asleep knowing Divine Guidance is mine. When the dawn comes, I am filled with peace. I go forth into the new day full of faith, confidence, and trust. Thank you, Father.

The Resurrection of My Desire

My desire for health, harmony, peace, abundance, and security is the voice of God speaking to me. I definitely choose to be happy and successful. I am guided in all ways. I open my mind and heart to the influx of the Holy Spirit; I am at peace. I draw successful and happy people into my experience. I recognize only the Presence and Power of God within me.

The Light of God shines through me and from me into everything about me. The emanation of God's Love flows from me; It is a healing radiance unto everyone who comes into my presence.

I now assume the feeling of being what I want to be. I know that the way to resurrect my desire is to remain faithful to my ideal, knowing that an Almighty Power is working in my behalf. I live in this mood of faith and confidence; I give thanks that it is done; for it is established in God, and all is well.

Achieving My Goal

In all thy ways acknowledge Him, and He will make plain thy path." My knowledge of God and the way He works is growing by leaps and bounds. I control and direct all my emotions along peaceful, constructive channels. Divine Love fills all my thoughts, words, and actions. My mind is at peace; I am at peace with all men. I am always relaxed and at ease. I know that I am here to express God fully in all ways. I believe implicitly in the guidance of the Holy Spirit within. This Infinite Intelligence within me now reveals to me the perfect plan of expression; I move toward it confidently and joyously. The goal and the objective that I have in my mind is good and very good. I have definitely planted in my mind the way of fulfillment. The Almighty Power now moves in my behalf; He is a Light on my path.

Business Problems

I know and believe my business is God's business; God is my partner in all my affairs; to me this means His light, love, truth, and inspiration fill my mind and heart in all ways. I solve all of my problems by placing my complete trust in the Divine Power within me. I know that this Presence sustains everything. I now rest in security and peace. This day I am surrounded by perfect under-standing; there is a Divine solution to all my problems. I definitely understand everyone; I am understood. I know that all my busi-ness relationships are in accord with the Divine Law of Harmony. I know that God indwells all of my customers and clients. I work harmoniously with others to the end that happiness, prosperity, and peace reign supreme.

Principle in Business

My business is God's business. I am always about my Father's business which is to radiate Life, Love, and Truth to all mankind. I am expressing myself fully now; I am giving of my tal-ents in a wonderful way. I am Divinely compensated.

God is prospering my business, profession, or activity in a wonderful way. I claim that all those in my organization are spiritual links in its growth, welfare, and prosperity; I know this, believe it, and rejoice that it is so. All those connected with me are Divinely prospered and illumined by the Light.

The Light that lighteth every man that cometh into the world leads and guides me in all ways. All my decisions are controlled by Divine Wisdom. Infinite Intelligence reveals better ways in which I can serve humanity. I rest in the Lord forever.

How to Solve Your Problems

What things soever you desire, when you pray, believe that ye receive them, and ye shall have them." I know that a problem has its solution within it in the form of a desire. The realization of my desire is good and very good. I know and believe that the Creative Power within me has the absolute Power to bring forth that which I deeply desire. The Principle which gave me the desire is the Principle which gives it birth. There is absolutely no argument in my mind about this.

I now ride the white horse which is the spirit of God moving upon the waters of my mind. I take my attention away from the problem and dwell upon the reality of the fulfilled desire. I am using the Law now. I assume the feeling that my prayer is answered. I make it real by feeling the reality of it. In Him I live, move, and have my being; I live in this feeling and give thanks.

Steps to Success

"W ist ye not that I be about my Father's business." I know that my business, profession, or activity is God's business. God's business is always basically successful. I am growing in wisdom and understanding every day. I know, believe, and accept the fact that God's law of abundance is always working for me, through me, and all around me.

My business or profession is full of right action and right expression. The ideas, money, merchandise, and contacts that I need are mine now and at all times. All these things are irresistibly attracted to me by the law of universal attraction. God is the life of my business; I am Divinely guided and inspired in all ways. Every day I am presented with wonderful opportunities to grow, expand, and progress. I am building up goodwill. I am a great success, because I do business with others, as I would have them do it with me.

The Triumph of Prayer

I now let go of everything; I enter into the realization of peace, harmony, and joy. God is all, over all, through all, and all in all. I lead the triumphant life, because I know that Divine Love guides, directs, sustains, and heals me. The Immaculate Presence of God is at the very center of my being; It is made manifest now in every atom of my body. There can be no delay, impediment, or obstructions to the realization of my heart's desire. The Almighty Power of God is now moving in my behalf. "None shall stay its hand, and say unto it, 'What doest thou?'" I know what I want; my desire is clear-cut and definite. I accept it completely in my mind. I remain faithful to the end. I have entered into the silent inner knowing that my prayer is answered and my mind is at peace.

How to Use the Power of Prayer

This book consists of ten of the most popular lessons from Dr. Murphy's radio programs, and is designed to give you a fundamental, basic, overall grasp of the essence of practical, mental laws. Each lesson reveals to you, how you can use the healing power, and attain the deepest desires of your heart.

He is an internationally known author, teacher, and lecturer. Thousands have heard him lecture and have been benefited by his tried and tested teachings.

Most of the common problems in everyday life he has had to meet, and now shows you in a simple, direct manner how you can solve your problems, and lead a more full, and happy life.

"He that dwelleth in the secret place of the most High shall abide under the shadow of the Almighty."

Dedicated to:

Robert
who is in favour with God and man.

Contents

1 How Your Mind Heals You 51

2 Practice of the Presence of God 53

3 Change Fear to Faith 55

4 Overcome Worry 59

5 Desire, the Gift of God 61

6 Happy Marriage 63

7 The Secret of Peace of Mind 65

8 You Can Have a Better Future 67

9 Overcome Irritation 69

10 Your Spiritual Rebirth 71

1

How Your Mind Heals You

There is a Healing Presence within you which heals all manner of disease. To use this Healing Presence requires knowledge of God, and the way He works.

Spiritual healing refers to wholeness, completeness, and perfection.

Science means knowledge of laws and principles; it means systematized and coordinated knowledge.

Knowledge of this Healing Principle is taken directly from the Bible. The means by which we unlock the mysteries, and reveal the hidden meaning of the Bible from Genesis to Revelation is the science of symbology and the science of the Hebrew alphabet.

The Bible deals with spiritual and mental laws. It recognizes the fact that many of the characters, such as Jesus, Moses, Elijah, Paul, and others were real men who lived on earth; nevertheless, they also represent states of mind within all of us. The Bible is a spiritual and psychological textbook.

Through the study and application of mental laws, *you* can find the way to health, harmony, peace, and prosperity; scientific prayer is the practice of the Presence of God.

Three Steps In Healing

The first step: Think of God as the only Presence and the only Power; God is a universal, creative Spirit present everywhere—the Living Spirit Almighty fixed in your own heart. Dwell on some of the things you know to be true about God; say quietly, for example: "He is Infinite Intelligence, Absolute Goodness, Infinite Power, Indescribable Beauty, Boundless Love, Infinite Wisdom, and All Powerful."

The second step: Forgive everyone; send loving thoughts to the whole world. Say, "I fully and freely forgive *everyone* now, and I go free." Add sincerely from your heart, "I mean this; it is true." You do not have any mental reservations.

The third step: Claim calmly and lovingly that the Infinite Healing Presence of God within you is now healing your body, making it whole, pure, and perfect. Declare to yourself, "I believe this; I accept it; I know the healing is taking place now." Give thanks for the harmony and peace that are yours.

"God in the midst of you is mighty to heal."

2

Practice of the Presence of God

The Omnipresence of God, means that God is present at every moment of time and every point of space. To practice the Presence of God all day long is the key to harmony, health, peace, joy, and a fullness of life. Begin now to see God in everyone and in everything.

The first step: Accept the fact that God is the only Presence and the only Power; He is the very Life and Reality of you.

The second step: Realize the Presence of God in all of the members of your family and in every person you meet. Salute the Divinity from this moment forward in everyone who crosses your path.

The third step: Realize, know, and claim that everything you are and everything you see, whether it is a tree, dog, or cat, is a part of God's expression; this is the greatest thing you can do; it is powerful beyond words.

Sit down quietly two or three times a day, and think along these lines: God is all there is; He is all in all. Begin to realize that the Divine Presence is within you and within everyone around you. *"Seek and you shall find. Seek ye first the Kingdom of God, and his righteousness; and all these things shall be added unto you."*

3

Change Fear To Faith

Whenever fear enters your mind, it is a signal for action; do something about it immediately; never surrender to your fear. Your fear is really a desire for something better; it is a longing for freedom and peace of mind. Where will you get your freedom and peace of mind? You will find it in the thoughts of peace, freedom, and poise.

If a man loses his way in the woods at night, fear seizes him; but knowing that God is all-wise, and knows the way out, he changes from fear to faith. He is now changing from the mood of fear to the mood of confidence and peace in the only Presence and the only Power. He has changed his mental attitude; this is often referred to as the Angel of God's Presence which leads him out into safety. The man who is lost turns to God in prayer and recognition, and says to himself quietly and lovingly, "God is guiding me now. He is a lamp unto my feet." He trusts and believes in this inner Light; this is the Light that lighteth every man that cometh into the world.

One with God is a majority! There is only fear and love. Fear is love in reverse. Love frees; it gives; it is the Spirit of God. Love builds the body. Love is also an emotional attachment. So fall in love with peace, gentleness, success, goodwill, and harmony, for this form of love casts out fear.

"God is love; and he that dwelleth in love dwelleth in God, and God in him."

Three Steps In Banishing Fear

The first step: "THE LORD is my light and my salvation; whom shall I fear? the LORD is the strength of my life; of whom shall I be afraid." *The Lord* means the Presence of God within you. There is no power to challenge God, for God is Almighty. The thing you fear has no power; it is a false belief; it is the bogey man under the stairs, and has no reality. Repeat these wonderful words: "God hath not given us the Spirit of fear; but of power, and of love, and of a sound mind."

The second step: You overcome fear by faith in God and all things good. Faith is not a creed, dogma, or a religion. Faith is a way of thinking; it is a positive, mental attitude. Faith is vital; it is a deep, abiding conviction in God. Faith is the greatest medicine in the world! Take this spiritual medicine of faith now! Look at these words; repeat them: "'I do all things through Christ which strengtheneth me.' God is with me now. God and His Holy Angels are always with me. I am surrounded by the circle of God's Love." These words are now reflected in your brain and deeper mind. Repeat these powerful statements, and all fear will leave you.

The third step: When fear thoughts come, think of God; imagine you are now resting in the arms of Almighty God in the same way as you rested in your loving mother's arms.

Say lovingly to your Father within, "Now, God, I am going about my business, and you are going with me. Your Love, Light, and Power comfort, guide, and bless me in all ways. I love my Father, and my Father loves me; my Father is God! It is wonderful!"

4

Overcome Worry

orry is due to a lack of faith in God. The person who worries is always expecting things to go wrong. They brood or worry over a great many things that never happen. Such a person tells you all of the reasons why something bad should happen, and not one reason why something good should happen. This constant worry debilitates their entire system, resulting in physical and mental disorders.

Your worry can be cured. Do not spend time looking at your troubles or problems; cease all negative thinking. Your mind will not work when it is tense. It relieves the strain to do something soothing and pleasant when you are presented with a problem. You do not fight a problem, but you can overcome it.

To release pressure, take a drive; go for a walk; play solitaire; read a favorite chapter of the Bible, such as: the eleventh chapter of Hebrews, or 1 Corinthians, 13; or turn to the forty-sixth Psalm; read it over carefully and quietly several times. An inner calm will steal over you, and you are ready to pray.

Steps In Overcoming Worry

The first step: Every morning when you awaken turn to God in prayer as you would to your loving Father. Relax the body; then talk to God, the only Presence and the only Power. Become as a little child; this means that you realize God is within you; you trust Him completely. "God in the midst of you is Mighty to heal."

The second step: You know in your heart that you can present your problems or difficulties to this Power, and that the Wisdom of God will solve it for you. Say lovingly: "Thank you, Father, for this wonderful day. It is God's day; it is filled with joy, peace, happiness, and success for me. I look forward with a happy expectancy to this day. The Wisdom and Understanding of God will govern me during the entire day. God is my partner; everything I do will turn out in a wonderful way. I believe in God; I trust God."

The third step: You are full of confidence and faith. Now let go; and let God work through you. Remember as you go through your day: "This is the day God made for me! There is Divine activity taking place in my life."

5

Desire—the Gift of God

God speaks to you through desire. All things begin with desire; it is sometimes called the fountain of all action. As you read this, you have within you the urge or desire to be greater than you are. There is a Cosmic urge within you seeking expression. Life seeks to express its unity, wholeness, love, and beauty through you. You are an instrument of the Divine; you are a channel for Life and Love. You are here to release the imprisoned splendor within you.

Without desire you could not move from your chair. Man desires shelter, and he proceeds to build houses to protect himself from the inclemencies of the season. Man plants seeds of corn and wheat in the ground, because he desires food for his family and himself.

You have a supreme desire now; perhaps it is for health, true place, or abundance. Desire unduly prolonged results in frustration and sickness. To desire something good and wonderful over a long period of time, and not attain it, is to waste away in spirit and body. You should learn to realize your desire through prayer; the realization of your desire is your saviour.

The Three Steps In Realizing Your Desire

The first step: Realizing your desire for harmony, peace, health, true place, wealth, etc., is the voice of God speaking to you. Say from your heart, "With God all things are possible." God is the Living Spirit Almighty within you from which all things flow.

The second step: I am aware of my desire; I know it exists in the Invisible for me. I claim it is mine now; I accept it in my own mind. I have released my desire into the Creative Medium within me, which is the source of all things. I claim and believe that my desire is now impressed in my deeper mind. What is impressed must be expressed; this is the way my mind works.

The third step: I now feel the reality of my fulfilled desire. I am at peace. I know in my heart what I have accepted as true will come to pass. I rejoice and give thanks. My whole being thrills to the reality of the fulfilled desire. I am at peace. God is peace. Thank you, Father, it is done.

6

Happy Marriage

W hat god hath joined together, let no man put asunder." A husband and wife should each be married to God and all things good. A husband and wife should never let the sun go down on their wrath. Never carry over from one day to another accumulated irritations arising from little disagreements. Be sure to forgive each other for any sharpness before you retire at night.

The answer to a happy marriage is for each one to see the Christ in the other; begin now to see the Presence of the Living God in each other. Say to yourself now, "I salute the Divinity in my husband or in my wife," as the case may be. Say to your wife or husband, "I appreciate all you are doing, and I radiate love and goodwill to you all day long." Do not take your marriage partner for granted; show your appreciation and your love.

Think appreciation and goodwill, rather than condemnation, criticism, and nagging. Remember the injunction of the Bible, "Except the Lord build the house, they labor in vain that build it." The way to build a peaceful home and a happy marriage is upon the basis of love, beauty, harmony, mutual respect, faith in God, and in all things good.

Say from your heart, "My marriage is consecrated in prayer and love." A husband and wife should always pray together at least once a day, preferably at night before retiring; this will restore peace in the home and in the heart; for God is peace.

Three Steps to a Happy Marriage

The first step: In the beginning God. The moment you awaken in the morning, claim God is guiding you in all ways. Send out loving thoughts of peace, harmony, and love to your marriage partner, to all members of the family, and to the whole world.

The second step: Say grace at breakfast. Give thanks for the wonderful food, for your abundance, and for all of your blessings. Make sure that no problem, worries, or arguments shall enter into the table conversation; the same applies at dinner time.

The third step: Husband and wife should alternate in praying each night. Keep the Bible close at hand. Read the 23rd, 91st, 27th Psalms, the 11th Chapter, Hebrews, the 13th Chapter, 1 Corinthians, and other great texts of the New Testament before going to sleep. Say quietly, "Thank you, Father, for all the blessings of the day. God giveth his beloved sleep."

7

The Secret of Peace of Mind

Communion with God is the way to peace of mind; this means turning to God in prayer and realizing that His Peace and Love are now flowing through your mind and heart. Prayer, or this silent communion with God within you, will change your character. Prayer makes you a different person.

The word *prayer* may be understood as including any form of communion with God whether vocal or mental. Peace of mind is achieved by getting a real sense of the Presence of God within you. In trying to bring peace into the lives of others, your personal opinion is usually wrong. By interfering in their strife, you usually make matters worse. By getting them to patch up their differences or arriving at a compromise to which they agree, there is no true peace, because they have not completely forgiven each other. The best way to heal quarrels of this nature is the silent way of prayer.

Realize the Wisdom, Love, and Peace of God are flowing through the minds and hearts of all concerned; the trouble will dissolve in a wonderful way. "Blessed are the peace makers; for they shall be called the children of God."

Three Steps to Peace of Mind

The first step: Realize God is Peace, and that He dwells in the midst of you; then think of that inner peace as yours now. Say quietly several times: "The Peace of God that passeth all understanding now floods my mind and heart."

The second step: Know that you have in your mind that which you constantly practice. Say frequently during the day, "I know that peace of mind is mine, because I enthrone thoughts of peace, harmony, and goodwill in my mind; I live with these ideas all day long."

The third step: Read the twenty third Psalm every night; relax the body; say, "I now enthrone in my mind thoughts of peace, love, and goodwill. God is my shepherd, and God's river of peace flows through me now. I lay me down in peace to sleep; for thou LORD, only maketh me dwell in safety."

8

You Can Have a Better Future

Remember what Paul said, "Faith without works is dead." You must demonstrate your faith. Faith is a way of thinking, an attitude of mind, a positive, affirmative approach toward life.

If you live, for example, in the joyous expectancy of the best, invariably the best will come to you.

You are demonstrating to the world that your faith is in all things good.

Live in the firm conviction of your oneness with God, with Life, and with the Universe. You will find yourself attracting to you wonderful people, greater prosperity, and increased awareness of God's Wisdom. Claim every day of your life that Divine Intelligence is directing your footsteps along the right path; know that God is your source of supply; He is the giver of every perfect gift. Realize that all of your needs are met, and that there is a Divine surplus.

To attain peace and harmony, say from your heart every morning as you arise, "God's peace, the peace that passeth all understanding, fills my mind and heart." Paul says that all things work together for good to them that love God. God and good are synonymous. You are in tune with all things Godlike, and behold, "If any man be in Christ, he is a new creature."

Three Steps to a Better Future

The first step: In all thy ways acknowledge Him, and He will make plain thy path, trust also in Him, and believe in Him, and He will bring it to pass. Turn to God within you; claim God is governing all of your affairs.

The second step: Realize the way to get along with people and adjust yourself to life is to love them. Let your heart be motivated by love and goodwill toward all around you. Pray for the peace and prosperity of all of those with whom you are associated.

The third step: Have a definite mental attitude of success. When presented with a problem, realize the Infinite Intelligence of God is revealing to you the perfect plan and showing you the way you should go. As you go to sleep say, "God knows the answer." Feel the joy of the answered prayer.

9

Overcome Irritation

He whose spirit is without restraint, is like a city that is broken down and without walls." "He that ruleth his spirit is greater than he that taketh a city."

In order that you might lead a full and happy life, control of the emotions is essential. To govern and control your emotions and temper tantrums, it is essential to maintain control over your thoughts. As a matter of fact you cannot find peace any other way. Will power or mental coercion will not do it. Forcing yourself to suppress your anger is not the way.

The answer is to enthrone God-like thoughts in your mind; busy yourself mentally with the concepts of peace, harmony, and goodwill. Keep firm control over your thoughts. Learn to substitute love for fear, and peace for discord.

You can direct your thoughts along harmonious lines. For example, if you see or hear of something that disturbs or angers you, instead of giving way to anger or irritation, say automatically, "The peace of God that passeth all understanding is now flooding my mind, my body, and my whole being." Repeat this phrase several times during the period of stress; you will find all tension and anger disappear.

Fill your mind with Love, and the negative thoughts cannot enter. When someone says something sharp or critical to you, think on a single statement of Truth, such as, "God is Love. He leadeth me beside the still waters." Peace steals over you; you will radiate this peace.

The Following Three Steps
Will Be Found Most Helpful

The first step: As you awaken in the morning, say to yourself: "This is God's day; it is a new day for me, a new beginning. The restoring, healing, soothing, loving power of God is flowing through me, bringing peace to my mind and body now and forevermore."

The second step: Should some business problem or some person upset or irritate you, think immediately about His Holy Presence. Say, "God is with me all day. His peace, His Guidance, and His Love enable me to meet all problems calmly and peacefully."

The third step: Radiate Love to all of your associates. Claim they are doing their best. Say, "I wish them peace, harmony, and joy. I salute the God in them." And lo and behold, God and His Love come forth!

10

Your Spiritual Rebirth

When the storm of life disturbs you, and it appears that your ship is about to founder, remember that it is time for you to awaken to the Christ within. This is how you become reborn spiritually: Recall to mind that God is within you, the very life of you. "Closer is He than breathing, nearer is He than hands and feet." Realize that "With God all things are possible." Claim and know that the God-Power within you is able to cope with any difficulty. Dwell on the peace and harmony of God where the difficulty is, and a perfect, Divine solution will follow.

If troubled say, "Peace be still!" The peace of God will steal over you. Turn your burdens (your problems) over to the God-Wisdom within you, knowing and believing that the perfect solution will come to you in God's own way. When you do this with faith and confidence, the storm or anxiety will pass away, and a great calm will steal over you; this is the peace that passeth all understanding. If you are living in limitation and sickness, this is bondage and restriction; it means you are in the dark as to the higher side of life and your tremendous potentialities. When you catch a glimpse of a higher set of facts, the old way of thinking will be displaced; then your Christ or inner Life will rise from the dead or limited state.

Enthrone the concept of peace, harmony, and success in your mind; busy your mind with these things; you will find your body and circumstances will reflect your inner, mental attitude; this is the new birth of freedom. Remove prejudices, deceit, and jealousies from your mind by opening your mind to the Light of God's Love and inspiration. God's Love revivifies and thrills you; this is the birth of God in you.

Three Steps To Your Spiritual Rebirth

The first step: "I saw a new heaven and a new earth." I know now that God's Love springs in my soul. My heart feels the Presence of God, because I radiate Love and joy to all.

The second step: Any time a negative, fearful, critical thought comes to me, I say, "God is with me." This kills it; then my soul is filled with Love toward all.

The third step: Remember always that God never changes. God is within you—your loving Father—Who is saying, "Fear not, child, for all is thine!"

About the Author

A native of Ireland who resettled in America, Joseph Murphy, Ph.D., D.D. (1898–1981) was a prolific and widely admired New Thought minister and writer, best known for his metaphysical classic, *The Power of Your Subconscious Mind*, an international bestseller since it first appeared on the self-help scene in 1963. A popular speaker, Murphy lectured on both American coasts and in Europe, Asia, and South Africa. His many books and pamphlets on the auto-suggestive and metaphysical faculties of the human mind have entered multiple editions—some of the most poignant of which appear in this volume. Murphy is considered one of the pioneering voices of affirmative-thinking philosophy.